A Note From Rick Renner

I am on a personal quest to see a "revival of the Bible" so people can establish their lives on a firm foundation that will stand strong and endure the test when the end-time storm winds begin to intensify.

In order to experience a revival of the Bible in your personal life, it is important to take time each day to read, receive, and apply its truths to your life. James tells us that if we will continue in the perfect law of liberty — refusing to be forgetful hearers but determined to be doers — we will be blessed in our ways. As you watch or listen to the programs in this series and work through this corresponding study guide, I trust that you will search the Scriptures and allow the Holy Spirit to help you hear something new from God's Word that applies specifically to your life. I encourage you to be a doer of the Word that He reveals to you. Whatever the cost, I assure you — it will be worth it.

> Thy words were found, and I did eat them;
> and thy word was unto me the joy and rejoicing of mine heart:
> for I am called by thy name, O Lord God of hosts.
> — Jeremiah 15:16

Your brother and friend in Jesus Christ,

Rick Renner

Reverence for the Things of God

How To Use This Study Guide

This five-lesson study guide corresponds to *"Reverence for the Things of God" with Rick Renner* (Renner TV). Each lesson in this study guide covers a topic that is addressed during the program series, with questions and references supplied to draw you deeper into your own private study of the Scriptures on this subject.

To derive the most benefit from this study guide, consider the following:

First, watch or listen to the program prior to working through the corresponding lesson in this guide. (Programs can also be viewed at **renner.org** by clicking on the Media/Archives links.)

Second, take the time to look up the scriptures included in each lesson. Prayerfully consider their application to your own life.

Third, use a journal or notebook to make note of your answers to each lesson's Study Questions and Practical Application challenges.

Fourth, invest specific time in prayer and in the Word of God to consult with the Holy Spirit. Write down the scriptures or insights He reveals to you about being filled with the Spirit and empowered by Him in your daily life.

Finally, take action! Whatever the Lord tells you to do according to His Word, do it.

For added insights on this subject, it is recommended that you obtain Rick Renner's book *The Will of God: The Key to Your Success*. You may also select from Rick's other available resources by placing your order at **renner.org** or by calling 1-800-742-5593.

TOPIC

Reverence for God in You

SCRIPTURES

1. **Psalm 139:14** — I will praise thee; for I am fearfully and wonderfully made: marvellous are thy works; and that my soul knoweth right well.
2. **Romans 1:7** — To all that be in Rome, beloved of God, called to be saints....
3. **1 Corinthians 6:19** — What? know ye not that your body is the temple of the Holy Ghost which is in you, which ye have of God, and ye are not your own?
4. **2 Corinthians 4:7** — But we have this treasure in earthen vessels, that the excellency of the power may be of God, and not of us.

GREEK WORDS

1. "saints/holy" — ἁγίοις (*hagios*): separated, consecrated, holy, and sacred — never again to be regarded or used in a common way; anything "holy" is in a category that is separate and sacred from other things
2. "temple" — ναός (*naos*): a temple or a highly decorated shrine; it presents the image of vaulted ceilings, marble, granite, gold, silver, and highly decorated ornamentation; pictures the most sacred, innermost part of a temple; the Holy of Holies
3. "we have" — ἔχω (*echo*): to have, hold, embrace, possess
4. "treasure" — θησαυρός (*thesauros*): describes a treasure, treasury, treasure chamber, or place of safekeeping where riches and fortunes were kept; presents the idea of a specially built room designed to be the repository for massive riches and wealth
5. "earthen vessels" — ὀστράκινος (*ostrakinos*): pictures pottery made of inferior materials; fragile pottery; the word generally represented anything inferior, low-grade, mediocre, shoddy, second-rate, or substandard; pottery that was used for casting votes against citizens who were banished from society; as a result, it meant to ostracize; where we get the word "ostracize"

SYNOPSIS

The five lessons in this study on *Reverence for the Things of God* will focus on the following topics:

- Reverence for God in You
- Reverence for God in the Church
- Reverence for God in the Bible
- Reverence for God in Tithes and Offerings
- Reverence for God in His People

The emphasis of this lesson:

You are the holy sanctuary of the presence of God. Although your body is relatively weak, fragile, and even defective in places, the Lord chose to deposit the inexhaustible riches of His Spirit inside you.

One of the most sacred places on earth is the Temple Mount in the ancient city of Jerusalem. For centuries upon centuries, these grounds have been treasured as holy. In fact, the Holy of Holies, which was the innermost sanctuary of the temple, was the place where the manifest presence of God dwelt. Priests and worshipers alike understood that going to the temple was a serious and reverent event never to be taken lightly.

Today, we are the temple in which the Spirit of God dwells (*see* 1 Corinthians 6:19). His very presence abides in each believer, making us His holy sanctuary. Accordingly, we must learn to be careful to honor and reverence God's presence in our lives. This starts and continues with having a clear understanding of who we are in Christ and keeping ourselves uncontaminated from the things of this world.

How Does God See You?

How you see yourself is very important to every aspect of your life. Although you are not to think of yourself more highly than others (*see* Romans 12:3), you are also not to think of yourself as worthless. God's Word says that you are "fearfully and wonderfully made" (*see* Psalm 139:16). He wants you to see yourself the way that He sees you.

The truth is, the moment you accept Jesus Christ as your Lord and Savior, God sees you as a "saint." Writing under the inspiration of the Holy Spirit, the apostle Paul said, "To all that be in Rome, beloved of God, called to be *saints…*" (Romans 1:7). Not only was he speaking to First-Century believers in Rome, but also to believers everywhere in every generation. Friend, you too are a "saint" in God's eyes!

The word "saints" in Romans 1:7 is a translation of the Greek word *hagios*, which means *separated, consecrated, holy, and sacred — never again to be regarded or used in a common way.* This word indicates that anything "holy" is in a category that is separate and sacred from other things. Thus, as a believer, you are *separated, consecrated, holy, and sacred* in God's eyes — nothing about you is common or ordinary. Friend, you can — and should — say what God says about you:

- "I am a saint; I am separated, consecrated, holy, and sacred to God."
- "I am fearfully and wonderfully made in His image!"

God's Word Is 'Holy'

An example of the word "holy" — translated here as *hagios* — is seen in the title given to the Scriptures. From its earliest formation, the Bible's full name has been *the Holy Bible.* This inscription still appears printed on many of the covers of today's copies of Scripture.

The word "Bible" is a translation of the Greek word *biblios*, which simply means *book* or *a scroll of writing.* However, when the word "holy" — the Greek word *hagios* — is placed in front of the word "Bible," it means that the Scriptures are *separated, consecrated, holy, sacred,* and *never to be regarded or used in a common way.* Anything that is "holy" is in a category that is separate and sacred from other things.

Thus, the *Holy Bible* is a special book that's set apart from all other books. It is so different that no other book in the world that has ever been written compares to it. If you walk into a library, you can probably find a copy of the *Holy Bible* on its shelves. Even though it is located among thousands of books, the word "holy" in the name "Holy Bible" signifies that it is in a category all by itself. And every time you call that precious Book by its name, you are affirming that it is like no other book — you set it apart into a special, consecrated, holy category that is different from all the other books. God's holy presence abides in His Word.

The Mount Where Moses Met God Is 'Holy'

Another example of this word "holy" is found in Exodus 3. When Moses approached the burning bush on the mountain of Horeb (also called Sinai), God told him to remove his shoes because he was standing on "holy" ground (*see* vs. 5). The word "holy" in the Septuagint version of this verse is also a translation of the Greek word *hagios*, and it tells us that God consecrated and sanctified that mountain.

If you had been there and looked at that mountain, you would have thought it looked no different than any other mountains in the region. Although there was nothing particularly unique about that mountain in terms of its appearance compared to other mountains, *God's presence had touched it.* And in that moment, His divine presence supernaturally separated that mountain from all other mountains and set it apart into a holy category.

It became so sacred at that moment that it became known as the *holy mount.* Though it was nestled as one mountain in the midst of an entire mountain range of normal mountains, it ceased to be normal from that day forward. God's presence had changed its status. It was now made holy and separated from all the rest.

Are you beginning to see how God sees you? The reason He calls you a "saint" — the Greek word *hagios* — is because His divine presence has touched your life and forever changed it. In fact, His presence has not only touched your life, His presence has taken up residence in your life. Your status is different from those in the world who have not committed and submitted to His lordship.

You Are God's Temple

In First Corinthians 6:19, the apostle Paul posed this question to the Corinthian believers — and to you: "What? know ye not that your body is the temple of the Holy Ghost which is in you, which ye have of God, and ye are not your own?"

The word "temple" is the Greek word *naos*, and it describes *a temple or a highly decorated shrine; it is the image of vaulted ceilings, marble, granite, gold, silver, and highly decorated ornamentation.* Specifically, this is the most sacred, innermost part of a temple; it is the word used in the Old Testament to describe the Holy of Holies.

Because you are a believer, *you are God's temple*. When you repented of sin and invited Jesus to be your Lord and Savior, His Holy Spirit moved into you and took up permanent residence. You are literally a walking, talking sanctuary of the Living God! This truth is so important it is repeated in First Corinthians 3:16 and again in Second Corinthians 6:16. What God says about you, you can — and should — say about you:

"I am God's temple — the Holy of Holies — where His Spirit permanently lives."

'X' Marks the Spot

Most likely you've read a story or seen a movie in which a person or group of people were searching for hidden treasure. The location of the treasure was usually specified on the map with a huge "X." Even today, treasure hunters are always scouring the earth looking for treasures and relics left by previous civilizations and generations.

Think of the great British archaeologist Howard Carter. In November of 1922, he discovered the intact tomb of the world renowned Egyptian Pharaoh known as King Tut. When he walked into that ancient burial chamber, his eyes beheld all the vast treasures of that young king that had been assembled and stored with him for centuries.

As immense and splendid as that discovery was, it is no match for the greatest treasure in the entire universe inside of you! As a child of God, you have a cache of wealth so massive that its reserves can never be completely dug out, explored, discovered, or discerned. These are spiritual assets beyond your wildest imagination!

In Second Corinthians 4:7, Paul said, "But we have this treasure in earthen vessels, that the excellency of the power may be of God, and not of us."

The phrase "we have" is the Greek word *echomen*, which is the plural form of the word *echo*. It means *to have, to hold, to embrace*, or *to possess*. It pictures someone who "has" something in his possession. It is rightfully his, and he has the right to keep it. Paul speaks in the plural, which indicates that he includes himself and all believers. The use of this word tells us that as born-again children of God, "We hold and possess as our very own" a "treasure."

The word "treasure" is the Greek word *thesauros*, and it describes *a treasure, a treasury, a treasure chamber*, or *a place of safekeeping where riches and fortunes are kept*. This word carries the idea of a specially built room designed to be the repository for massive riches and wealth. By using this term, Paul declared that we believers are the possessors of inexhaustible riches beyond belief. We are the *treasure chambers*, *repositories*, or *treasuries* where God has placed this fortune.

Because the word *echomen* precedes the word *thesauros*, this phrase could be translated as, "We have and hold this immense, inexhaustible wealth in our possession." In other words, it is not something we are trying to obtain — it is something we *already possess*. We are God's treasure chamber, and a spiritual "X" marks our lives as the place where He has deposited inexhaustible wealth.

We Are 'Earthen Vessels'

Paul went on to say that the vast treasure of God is stored in "earthen vessels" (2 Corinthians 4:7). The words "earthen vessels" is the Greek word *ostrakinos*, and it describes *pottery that was made of inferior materials; it was fragile and easily broken*. This kind of pottery was weak, valueless, and full of defects. It was so cheaply made that it would never have been seen in wealthier homes. Hence, these "bargain-basement" dishes were used in the lower-class neighborhoods, purchased by people who couldn't afford to acquire better merchandise.

If you would have visited an average Greek or Roman home in the First Century, you would have seen *ostrakinos* (earthen vessels) arranged on people's tables. These dishes were very inexpensive to buy and easily replaced if broken. People loved them because they were so beautifully decorated with colorful paint that their imperfections were adequately hidden.

As time passed, this word *ostrakinos* came to represent *anything inferior, low-grade, mediocre, shoddy, second-rate, or substandard*. It is also from where we get the phrase "to ostracize." When people "ostracize" a person, it means they regard him or her as *substandard* — too unfit to be a part of their group. They speak derogatorily of them, poke fun at them, and belittle them in front of others. The person being "ostracized" most likely feels as though he or she has been cut out of the group — shunned, ignored, and treated like something that is shoddy and deficient.

Interestingly, because this pottery was made of inferior, low-grade material that was easily broken, its shards were often used by citizens to cast votes. When an individual was placed on trial, citizens took a piece of this pottery and would write a name or a number on it, and by doing so, they would cast their vote, determining whether or not to banish the individual in question. Those that were banished were said to be "ostracized" from society.

Shoddy, deficient, substandard pottery is exactly the kind of "earthen vessels" Paul had in mind when he wrote Second Corinthians 4:7. The "earthen vessels" in which God has placed His treasure is our weak and fragile *human bodies*. Paul used the illustration of these cheaply made dishes to announce the location of the secret chamber where God placed His greatest treasure on planet earth. It's inside of us! If "X" marks the spot, then the "X" is marked on us!

Putting the meanings of all these words together, here is the *Renner Interpretive Version* (*RIV*) for 2 Corinthians 4:7:

> **We possess treasure within ourselves! And not only do we possess treasure, but our easily broken, inferior, temporary bodies are themselves the treasure chambers where this astonishing treasure is kept....**

Paul used these Greek words, almost in amazement, to joyfully announce that the human body is the residence of the Holy Spirit.

- A wrong diet can kill the body.
- Working too hard can break it.
- Too much pressure can damage it.
- And even after caring for it your entire lifetime, it still eventually dies.
- Yet God placed His greatest treasure inside us, anyway!

Friend, you are the hiding place for God's greatest treasure — the third Person of the Godhead, the Holy Spirit! Even though in the natural you may seem weak, defective, and valueless, God has chosen your human body as the place to hide His greatest treasure. Start embracing who He made you to be and reverence His presence in your life.

STUDY QUESTIONS

> **Study to shew thyself approved unto God, a workman that needeth not to be ashamed, rightly dividing the word of truth.**
> **— 2 Timothy 2:15**

1. Take a few moments to reread the meaning of the words "earthen vessels" — the Greek word *ostrakinos*. What is the Holy Spirit showing you about yourself through the use of this word?

2. When we sin and miss the mark of God's standard, we are often discouraged and surprised by our behavior. Interestingly, God is never shocked or caught off guard by what we do or say. How does Psalm 139:1-4 and verses 15 and 16 specifically confirm this to be true? (Also consider Psalm 56:8 and Jeremiah 1:5.)

3. In spite of our weak, fragile, and sometimes even defective frame — and our tendency to make mistakes — what will God never bring against us (*see* Romans 8:1,33,34 and John 3:17,18)? According to Romans 8:35-39, what has He promised us — even through life's difficulties and our own disobedience?

PRACTICAL APPLICATION

> But be ye doers of the word, and not hearers only,
> deceiving your own selves.
> —James 1:22

1. Be honest. What do you think about yourself? Do you *like* yourself or *loathe* yourself? What kinds of words or phrases usually come to your mind when you think of yourself?

2. If you are putting yourself down internally or speaking derogatorily about yourself, it's time to make some changes. Knowing that the power of life or death is in your tongue, what are some new, life-giving statements you can begin saying to yourself and about yourself? (Consider what God says about you in 2 Corinthians 5:17 and 21 and Ephesians 1:6.)

3. Knowing that you are a walking talking temple of God's Holy Spirit, is there any person, place, or thing He is showing you from which you need to separate yourself? If so, identify it.

TOPIC

Reverence for God in the Church

SCRIPTURES

1. **Hebrews 12:23** — To the general assembly and church of the firstborn, which are written in heaven, and to God the Judge of all, and to the spirits of just men made perfect.

2. **Revelation 1:13** — And in the midst of the seven candlesticks one like unto the Son of man, clothed with a garment down to the foot, and girt about the paps with a golden girdle.

3. **Revelation 2:1** — ...these things saith he that holdeth the seven stars in his right hand, who walketh in the midst of the seven golden candlesticks....

4. **Ephesians 5:26,27** — That he [Jesus] might sanctify and cleanse it [the Church] with the washing of water by the word, that he might present it to himself a glorious church, not having spot, or wrinkle, or any such thing; but that it should be holy and without blemish.

GREEK WORDS

1. "general assembly" — πανήγυρις (*paneguris*): from πᾶς (*pas*) and ἀγορά (*agora*); the word πᾶς (*pas*) means all, every, or every part, and it is all-encompassing; the word ἀγορά (*agora*) means the marketplace, a public forum, or even a location of public celebration; the word ἀγορά (*agora*) primarily refers to a public forum or gathering where trials were held, where products were sold, where ideas were exchanged, and where slaves were purchased; compounded, the new word presents the picture of a place where celebrations occur, laws and verdicts are issued, products and ideas are taught and exchanged, or slaves are purchased by a new owner

2. "church" — ἐκκλησία (*ekklesia*): a called, separated, and prestigious assembly; denotes a prestigious assembly of distinguished citizens who determined laws, debated public policy, formulated new policies, argued and ruled in judicial matters, and elected the chief magistrates of the land; to be selected from society and invited to join this assem-

bly was a great honor; in the New Testament, it depicts the body of believers who have been called out, called forth, selected, and assembled to be God's representatives in every town, city, state or nation; a body called to make decisions that affect the atmosphere of a region

3. "midst" — μέσος (*mesos*): right in the very center; right in the very midst or to be in the gut or heart of a thing

4. "garment down to the foot" — the description of the high priest in Exodus 28

5. "walketh" — περιπατέω (*peripateo*): to walk around; to live and carry on in one general vicinity; pictures one who has walked one path for so long that he can now almost walk that path blindfolded; this person knows this path because he has habitually lived and functioned there; denotes the movement of the feet; suggests one who has walked in one region for so long that it has now become his environment, his place of daily activity; often translated "to live"; to stroll

6. "golden" — χρυσός (*chrusos*): gold; the most valuable material that existed in the ancient world; denotes that which is rare and highly prized; pictures something precious and of great significance

SYNOPSIS

As we noted in Lesson 1, the Temple Mount in Jerusalem was and still is considered a holy, sacred place. As the people of Israel made their way toward the temple, they climbed a series of steps. But before they began their ascent, they went through a time of ceremonial cleansing in which they washed themselves in pools of water and put on white clothing to demonstrate that they had purified themselves and prepared their hearts.

With each upward step they took, these worshipers quoted Scripture and focused their mind on the Lord. They had a genuine reverence for God's temple knowing it was a place where His manifest presence dwelt. Unfortunately, many people today — especially in the western world — have very little reverence for God in the Church. Oftentimes the way we think, the way we dress, and how we behave often reveals a far too casual attitude.

Gathering together with fellow believers is very different from going to the grocery store, the shopping mall, or the bowling alley. It is a holy, sacred assembling where we unite in God's presence to be equipped, empowered, and directed into His will. Stop and ask yourself: *How do I prepare to experience God at church?*

The emphasis of this lesson:

As believers, we need to cultivate a sincere reverence for the presence of God in His Church. We must prepare our hearts and minds appropriately before entering His presence.

A Detailed Description of the Church

In Hebrews 12:23, the writer addresses the Church and describes it in some very unique ways. He said, "To the general assembly and church of the firstborn, which are written in heaven, and to God the Judge of all, and to the spirits of just men made perfect."

Notice the words "general assembly." In Greek, it is the word *paneguris*, which is a compound of the words *pas* and *agora*. The word *pas* means *all, every,* or *every part,* and it is *all-encompassing.* The word *agora* means *the marketplace, a public forum,* or even *a location of public celebration*; it primarily refers to *a public forum or gathering where trials were held, products were sold, ideas were exchanged, and slaves were purchased.* When the words *pas* and *agora* are compounded to form the word *paneguris*, it presents *the picture of a place where celebrations occur, a place where laws and verdicts are issued, where ideas are taught and products exchanged, and where slaves are purchased by a new owner.*

What does all this mean? It means the Church — described here as the "general assembly" — is a place of celebration where we come together to celebrate the presence of God. Second, it is a place where laws and verdicts are issued. Specifically, this signifies the public teaching of God's Word. Third, the Church is a place where ideas are exchanged. This includes the sharing of spiritual and practical ideas among God's people. Moreover, the Church is a place where people are purchased out of slavery to sin — a place where people get saved by the power of Jesus Christ.

This brings us to another very important word in Hebrews 12:23 — the word "church." This is the Greek word *ekklesia*, which is a compound of the word *ek*, meaning *out*, and a form of the word *kaleo*, meaning *to call* or *to beckon*. When these two words are compounded to form the word *ekklesia*, it describes *a called out, separated, and prestigious assembly.*

Interestingly, the word *ekklesia* was taken from the secular world of the Athenians. On a hill near the renowned Acropolis in the city of Athens, a prestigious group of six thousand citizens that had been selected and called out of society gathered regularly to determine laws, debate public policy, formulate new policies, argue and rule in judicial matters, and elect the chief magistrates of the land. To be selected from society and invited to join this assembly was a great honor.

In the New Testament, the word *ekklesia* — translated as "church" — depicts the body of believers who have been *called out, called forth, selected, and assembled to be God's representatives in every town, city, state or nation.* We are the Church. We are a body of believers called out by God *to make decisions that affect the atmosphere of the regions in which we live.* Indeed, it is a great honor to be invited into this prestigious assembly.

Jesus Is in the 'Midst' of the Church

Without question, the Church is extremely important in the mind of God. In fact, it is so important that Jesus Himself is described in the book of Revelation as standing in the midst of the Church. The apostle John described Jesus as being "…in the midst of the seven candlesticks one like unto the Son of man, clothed with a garment down to the foot, and girt about the paps with a golden girdle."

The word "midst" in this verse is the Greek word *mesos*, and it means *right in the very center, right in the very midst,* or *to be in the gut or heart of a thing.* This word is repeated several times throughout chapters 1 and 2 of Revelation.

Also notice the phrase "garment down to the foot." It describes how Jesus was dressed and is taken from the Greek word *poderes*, which is used seven times in the Greek Septuagint to describe the attire of the high priest. It depicts *a robe that flows all the way down to the ankles but leaves the feet exposed.* The reason the high priest didn't wear shoes was to prevent him from carrying the contamination of the world into the presence of God. Accordingly, before he went into the Holy of Holies, the high priest would remove his shoes.

Perhaps the best example of this word *poderes* is found in Exodus 28, where God told Moses how to make "holy garments" for Aaron and his sons, who would serve as priests. These priestly garments were to be made of gold, blue, purple, and scarlet thread and fine woven linen. Each robe was to reach down to the ankles, which is exactly like the robe Christ was wearing in John's vision.

The garment Jesus wore portrays Him as our Great High Priest. He is so reverent about the Church that He stands in its midst *prayerfully*. He doesn't stand outside the Church pointing out all of her faults and flaws. Neither does He stand mocking or criticizing it. In spite of her defects, He is standing in her very midst patiently and lovingly interceding for it.

Jesus Wore a 'Golden Girdle'

In addition to the flowing robe Jesus wore, the Bible says He was "…girt about the paps with a golden girdle" (Revelation 1:13). The word "paps" is the Greek word *mastros*, and it describes the *mid-to-upper-chest*. And the phrase "golden girdle" in Greek is *zoonen chrusan* — a compound of the words *zoone* and *chrusos*. The word *zoone* depicts *a girdle, belt*, or *waistband*. The word *chrusos* describes *pure gold*, the most valuable material that existed in the ancient world. It denotes *that which is rare and highly prized* and can be used figuratively to denote *something precious or of great significance*.

In the ancient world, belts were worn around the waist to tightly hold long, flowing garments together. But kings in the East wore belts of gold that were positioned high up on their chests to demonstrate power and wealth. This royal belt served as a symbol of *power, majesty, dignity*, and *authority*.

Worn on the king's mid-chest, the "golden girdle" was impossible to miss and designed to impress those who beheld it. In biblical times, there was no higher status symbol. Kings of lesser wealth and power wore belts around their mid-chest, but their belts were made of *strands* of gold woven together with other less valuable materials. The cost was simply too high for a lesser king to own a belt made of pure gold.

So when a king displayed a belt of pure gold on his upper body, onlookers would know that this was a king with immense wealth, power, and authority. The fact that Jesus is depicted in the midst of the Church with a "golden girdle" shows His *power, majesty, dignity, authority*, and *vast resources*.

This golden girdle portrayed Jesus as a *King* possessing unimaginable greatness. His belt of pure gold around His upper mid-chest reminds us that He holds ultimate power over all the affairs of the earth — including human rulers, governments, and the Church — over which He rules as Head, King, and Lord.

The Church Is Christ's Habitation

The apostle John went on to tell us that Jesus "...walketh in the midst of the seven golden candlesticks" (Revelation 2:1). We know from Revelation 1:20 that the "seven golden candlesticks" refer to the *seven major churches* located on the continent of Asia. At the same time, they also signify the Church as a whole. Thus, Jesus is walking back and forth inside the Church.

The word "walketh" is a translation of the Greek word *peripateo*, which is a compound of the word *peri*, meaning *around*, and the word *pateo*, meaning *to walk*. When the two words come together to form the word *peripateo*, it means *to walk around; to live and carry on in one general vicinity*. It is a picture of one who has walked one path for so long that he can now almost walk that path blindfolded. This person knows this path because he has habitually lived and functioned there.

The word *peripateo* also denotes *the movement of the feet*; it suggests one who has walked in one region for so long that it has now become his environment, his place of daily activity. It is often translated *to live* or *to stroll*. Therefore, when the Bible says that Jesus "walketh in the midst of the seven golden candlesticks," it means that He lives in the very center of the Church; it has become His habitation.

It is important to note that Jesus sees the Church as "golden." The apostle John noted this in Revelation 1:20 and 2:1. The word "golden" is the Greek word *chrusos*, which in Scripture describes *the purest and highest quality of gold*. Although there were other forms of gold, they were inferior because they were mixed with other alloys. When Jesus looks at the Church, He sees it as pure gold — *chrusos* — the most valuable and desirable form of gold that existed in the ancient world.

Becoming 'Golden' Is a Heated and Intense Process

Interestingly, the majority of available gold is located in rock that must be mined from the earth, and the process of extracting it has always been long and expensive. First, the rock must be removed from the earth and then crushed into dust. Once the rock is crushed, tons of water is used to wash away the lighter rock and dirt, leaving behind the heavier raw gold. The gold is then gathered and placed into a furnace with blazing hot temperatures that melt it into liquid form.

In the fire, the molten gold bubbles under the heat of the blaze, and unsightly impurities called "slag" or "dross" begin to rise to the surface. As they do, the refiner carefully scrapes them off. This process is repeated again and again — each time using a hotter furnace — until all impurities are exposed and removed and the only substance left is *pure* gold.

The heat required to produce pure gold is intense. From beginning to end, the refining process is tedious, expensive, uncomfortable, and complicated — but it is the only way to produce the *purest gold*. Eliminating the impurities in gold was impossible without fire. Nevertheless, once the process is complete, pure gold is produced that can be shaped into any object.

It was this type of gold that was used to make all the instruments for the holiest part of God's temple — the Holy of Holies. In the ancient world, only pure gold was fitting for powerful kings or nobility. When ambassadors or the head of a foreign state came to visit a king, they came with gifts of gold (*chrusos*) to show respect and honor.

The use of the word "golden" in Revelation 1:12 and 2:1 conveys the *immense value* that Jesus Christ places on His Church. It is vital for us to see and understand this — especially in our age when so much criticism is leveled against the Body of Christ and when so many people focus on our failures and weaknesses. Remember, Jesus gave His own blood to purchase the Church, which includes you. In doing so, He clearly demonstrated how *valuable* and *precious* you are to Him.

The Church Is Being Refined

Friend, Jesus is still in the process of purifying the Church. He is the Refiner who sits and watches over our purification and refinement. The Church's imperfections are nothing new. As long as we await the coming of Jesus, this refining process will never end. Amazingly, regardless of our imperfections, He still sees us — His Church — as *pure gold*.

Throughout the process of refinement, the Spirit's fire is working to expose all blemishes in order to bring the Church to a higher level of purification. You may feel disheartened by what you see or know about the Church. You may even be discouraged because of experiences with a local body of believers. But remember, Jesus loves His Church and He bought it with His own life's blood. When you see the unsightly blemishes in His people, realize it is a sign that He is actively at work bringing these impurities to the surface so that He can remove them.

Ephesians 5:26 and 27 speaks of Jesus' purifying work, telling us His purpose and goal through it all. It says, "That he [Jesus] might sanctify and cleanse it [the Church] with the washing of water by the word, that he might present it to himself a glorious church, not having spot, or wrinkle, or any such thing; but that it should be holy and without blemish."

So if you're tempted to focus on the imperfections in the Church — or even in yourself — think back to the refining process and all the impurities that Christ, the Refiner, is scraping off the surface. He has removed His shoes, put on His robe, and taken on the role of our eternal High Priest. He is walking up and down in the center of the Church praying for it and purifying it. He is not blind to the defects you see. He is just patiently working in us and through us to produce the finest pure gold the world will ever see. If Jesus respects and loves His Church, then so should we.

STUDY QUESTIONS

Study to shew thyself approved unto God, a workman that needeth not to be ashamed, rightly dividing the word of truth.
— 2 Timothy 2:15

1. After reading through the original Greek meanings of the words "general assembly" and "church," how has your understanding of the Body of Christ been expanded? What new facets of the Church do you now see that you didn't see before? For what reasons do you personally consider it an *honor* to be a part of God's *ekklesia* (the Church)?

2. The Bible says that Jesus is standing in the midst of the Church wearing a "golden girdle," showing His *power, majesty,* and *authority* (*see* Revelation 1:13). How do Ephesians 1:20-23; Philippians 2:9-11; and Colossians 2:15 explain the meaning of this truth? (Also consider Matthew 28:18.) How does this strengthen your faith?

3. According to Philippians 1:6 and 2:13 and First Thessalonians 5:23 and 24, what is God's part in the transformation and refinement of your life? (Also consider 2 Corinthians 3:18.)

PRACTICAL APPLICATION

But be ye doers of the word, and not hearers only,
deceiving your own selves.
— James 1:22

1. From your perspective, how is going to church different than going to a movie theater or a sporting event? What kinds of things do you do to prepare for church that set it apart as a special, sacred experience?

2. When Jesus looks at His Church, He sees it as "golden" (*see* Revelation 1:20). When you look at the Church, how do you see it? Is it as an institution filled with flaws *or* the Body of Christ? Is it just a building where people go on Sundays to do their duty *or* is it holy ground where the presence of God Himself dwells and manifests as He meets with those He loves dearly?

LESSON 3

TOPIC

Reverence for God in the Bible

SCRIPTURES

1. **Psalm 119:105** — Thy word is a lamp unto my feet, and a light unto my path.

2. **Joshua 1:7** — … turn not from it to the right hand or to the left hand, that thou mayest prosper whithersoever thou goest.

3. **2 Timothy 3:16** — All scripture is given by inspiration of God, and is profitable for doctrine, for reproof, for correction, for instruction in righteousness: that the man of God may be perfect, throughly furnished unto all good works.

GREEK WORDS

1. "all" — **πᾶσα** (*pasa*): all, with no part excluded; every bit of it; each and every part

2. "scripture" — **γραφή** (*graphe*): used 51 times in the New Testament to describe the Old and New Testament scriptures

3. "inspiration" —Θεόπνευστος (*theopneustos*); from Θεός (*theos*) and πνέω (*pneo*); the word Θεός (*theos*) means God; the word πνέω (*pneo*) means "to breathe"; also the Old Testament word for creative power, for air blown from the mouth into a wind instrument to produce music, and for perfume; God breathed the Scriptures, and it released creative power, a new sound of music, and a new, God-imparted fragrance

4. "profitable" — ὠφέλιμος (*ophelimos*): helpful, profitable, useful, beneficial; something that is to one's advantage; can be translated as "needful" or "obligatory"; mandatory; essential; an absolute requirement

5. "for" — πρός (*pros*): toward; face to face; can also mean "to confront"

6. "doctrine" — διδασκαλία (*didaskalia*): doctrine; well-packaged teaching with application to living; teaching that applies to and affects one's life

7. "reproof" — ἔλεγχος (*elegchos*): to expose, to convict, or to cross-examine for the purpose of conviction, as when convicting a lawbreaker in a court of law; the image of a lawyer who brings evidence that is indisputable and undeniable, so the accused person's actions are irrefutably brought to light and the offender is exposed and convicted; used to denote a lawyer who worked to convince people of a new way of thinking or a new way of seeing things

8. "correction" — ἐπανόρθωσις (*epanorthosis*): to correct; to set straight; to erect; to set upright or cause to be level; an action that picks one up and sets him upright on his feet again

9. "instruction" — παιδεία (*paideia*): to train, educate, or to give a child everything necessary to prepare him for life; child training; the process of getting a child ready for life so that afterward, he can be sent out fully equipped and successfully live as he was taught and trained to do; the term for all types of essential instruction, both for children and adults

10. "righteousness" — δικαιοσύνη (*dikaiosune*): right living; epitomizes those who live by a righteous standard that results in upright living

11. "perfect" — ἄρτιος (*artios*): complete; mature; adequate; completely sufficient in every way

12. "thoroughly furnished" — ἐξαρτίζω (*exartidzo*): to completely deck out; to fully supply; to fully equip; depicts a ship that had previously been ill-equipped for traveling, but was now loaded with new equipment and gear that enabled it to sail anywhere; such boats were fully supplied, completely equipped, or thoroughly furnished; depicts a boat

equipped to make it through all kinds of weather, including strong storms; a boat equipped for long-distance sailing

SYNOPSIS

In Old Testament times, the people of Israel faithfully came to the temple in Jerusalem to experience the presence of God and to worship Him. These were very sacred encounters for them — so sacred that they took the time to purify themselves, prepare their hearts, and put together an offering to present to the Lord at the temple.

What's interesting is the vital role the Scriptures played as they readied themselves to enter God's presence and made their way up the steps toward the temple. These worshipers had invested time and effort to memorize the psalms, and with each step they took, they would pause and sing an entire psalm. Without question, they had great reverence for God and His Word.

In Lesson 1, we studied the importance of having a reverence for God in *us* — the temple of His Holy Spirit. In Lesson 2, we focused on the need of reverencing God in *His Church*. In this lesson, we will concentrate on cultivating a reverence for God in *the Bible*.

The emphasis of this lesson:

The Bible is not just a book that tells us about God. It is His Living Word filled with God Himself. When we open it and reverently take it in, it releases His presence and power within us.

There's No Book Like the Bible

The Bible is the most powerful, life-changing book on the face of the earth. Although kings have banned it, tyrants have burned it, and many have lost their lives as they sought to preserve it for the next generation, it still remains the best-selling book of all time.

Sadly, millions of people who "profess Christ" never read their Bibles. In poll after poll, Christians admit that they do not study the Scriptures. If you entered their homes, most likely you'd find a Bible in the bathroom, the bedroom, the kitchen, and even the living room, but they would be unread and gathering dust. Statistics reveal that even many pastors don't read their Bibles unless they are preparing a message.

Friend, you need the Holy Bible in your life! In Psalm 119:105, David said, "Thy word is a lamp unto my feet, and a light unto my path." When the Word is regularly hidden in your heart, it helps you avoid falling into sin (*see* Psalm 119:11). When it is received in humility, it has the power to save your soul (*see* James 1:21). You may read many books during your lifetime, but the Bible is the only book that reads you. It is no wonder that the Lord spoke to Joshua as he began to lead the nation of Israel and said:

> **This Book of the Law shall not depart from your mouth, but you shall meditate in it day and night that you may observe to do according to all that is written in it. For then you will make your way prosperous, and then you will have good success**
> **—Joshua 1:8 *NKJV***

Think about it. The Bible contains the mind of God, the condition of man, the way of salvation, the judgment of sinners, and the happiness of believers. Its doctrines are holy, its truths are binding, its histories are true, and its decisions are unchangeable. It is the traveler's map, the pilot's compass, and the soldier's sword. Read it to be wise. Believe it to be safe. Practice it to be holy. It should fill your memory, rule your heart, and guide your feet. Read it slowly, read it frequently, read it prayerfully. Your obedience to it is your highest responsibility.

'All Scripture Is Given by Inspiration of God'

One of the most important verses about the Bible in the New Testament is found in Second Timothy 3:16. Writing under the inspiration of the Holy Spirit, the apostle Paul said, "All scripture is given by inspiration of God, and is profitable for doctrine, for reproof, for correction, for instruction in righteousness." This verse is simply filled with truth that we need to know.

First, notice the word "all." It is the Greek word *pasa*, and it indicates *all, no part excluded; every bit of it; each and every part.* Thus, every bit of Scripture — not one part excluded — is given by inspiration of God.

The word "scripture" is the Greek word *graphe*, and it is used 51 times in the New Testament to describe *the full body of the Old and New Testament scriptures.* All Scripture — every dotted "i" and every crossed "t" — is given by inspiration of God.

This brings us to the word "inspiration," which is the Greek word *theopneustos*, a compound of the words *theos* and *pneuo*. The word *theos* means

God and is from where we get the word *theology*, which is *the study of God.* The word *pneuo* means *to breathe.* When these two words are compounded to form the word *theopneustos*, it means that all Scripture is *God-breathed.*

How did God give us the Scriptures? The answer is found in Second Peter 1:20 and 21. It says, "...No prophecy of scripture is of any private interpretation. For the prophecy came not in old time by the will of man: but holy men of God spake as they were moved by the Holy Ghost." So as the Holy Ghost moved on men, they began to write what He put in their hearts and minds. Again and again, the Spirit of God breathed out truth over a span of about 1,500 years, and men continued to write until all the Scriptures were completed.

Three Dynamic Meanings for the Word 'Inspiration'

Let's look once again at the Greek word *theopneustos* — the word translated as "inspiration." We saw that it is a compound of the word *theo,* meaning *God,* and the word *pneustos,* which is from the word *pnéō,* meaning *to breathe.* What you may not know is that there are three additional historical meanings of the word *pneuo* in the Old Testament and secular literature that are very important.

First, the word *pneuo* was the Old-Testament word for *creative power.* This word was used in Genesis 1 to describe the Spirit of God as He moved upon the face of the deep and began to create the world.

Second, the word *pneuo* was the word used to describe *the air that is blown from the mouth into a wind instrument to produce music.* An example of this is a musician placing a French horn on his lips, inhaling and filling his lungs with air, and then blowing the air through the horn to produce music. This is a demonstration of the word *pneuo.*

Third, the word *pneuo* was *the ancient word for perfume.* These three meanings tell us that when God breathed the Scriptures, He released *creative power,* produced *a new sound of music,* and emitted *a new God-imparted fragrance.*

What does all this mean to you personally? It means if you don't like what's going on in your life, open your Bible and it will begin to release creative power to change your situations. If you don't like what you're hearing, get into the Word and release its power, and it will bring new sounds into your life. And if you don't like the stinking circumstances in your home, your finances, or your relationships, open the Bible and let the

Word release its power to bring a fresh new fragrance into every area of your life. All of this meaning is found in this phrase, "given by the inspiration of God," the Greek word *theopneustos*.

All Scripture Is 'Profitable'

In addition to being "God-breathed," all Scripture "…is profitable…" (2 Timothy 3:16). The Greek word for "profitable" means *helpful, profitable, useful, beneficial; something that is to one's advantage*. It can also be translated as *needful* or *obligatory*; something that is *mandatory, essential*, or *an absolute requirement*. This lets us know that Scripture is *not* optional in our lives — it is absolutely mandatory. If you want to release creative power, bring the sounds of Heaven, and experience God's life-changing aroma in your life, you must have the Word.

The Scriptures are profitable for "doctrine." The word "doctrine" is the Greek word *didaskalia*, which is from the word *didasko*, meaning *to teach*. In this case, the word *didaskalia* describes *well-packaged teaching that applies to and affects one's life*. Also notice the word "for" in Second Timothy 3:16. It appears four times, and it is the Greek word *pros*, which carries the idea of a *confrontation*. When you read the Bible, the truth will *confront* you and bring you to a place where you see what you need to see about yourself face-to-face.

The Scriptures are profitable for "reproof." The word "reproof" is the Greek word *elegchos*, and it means *to expose, to convict*, or *to cross-examine for the purpose of conviction, as when convicting a lawbreaker in a court of law*. It is the image of a lawyer who brings evidence that is indisputable and undeniable so that the accused person's actions are irrefutably brought to light, and the offender is exposed and convicted. This word was also used to denote a lawyer who worked to convince people of a new way of thinking or a new way of seeing things. Thus, the Word of God has the innate ability to expose areas of our lives and bring indisputable evidence that convicts us and helps us see where we need to change.

The Scriptures are profitable for "correction." The word "correction" is the Greek word *epanorthosis*, which means *to correct, to set straight, to erect, to set upright*, or *cause to be level*. It describes *an action that picks one up and sets him upright on his feet again after having been previously knocked down in life*. This means when life is harsh, harmful, and emotionally hard to bear and you've been knocked flat by disappointments and difficulties, the Word of God can resurrect you back to life again if you will fully embrace it.

The Scriptures are profitable for "instruction in righteousness." The word "instruction" here is a translation of the Greek word *paideia*, which means *to train* or *educate a child and give him or her everything necessary to prepare them for life*. It describes *child training* or *the process of getting a child ready for life so afterward he can be sent out fully equipped and successfully live as he was taught and trained to do*. This brings us to the word "righteousness," which is the Greek word *dikaiosune*, and it describes *upright* or *right living*. It epitomizes those who live by a righteous standard that results in upright living.

Putting the meanings of all these words together, here is the *Renner Interpretive Version* (*RIV*) of 2 Timothy 3:16:

> **All scripture — each and every bit of it and not a part of it excluded — has been breathed from the mouth of God and carries creative power, beautiful new heavenly sounds, and is filled with a divine fragrance to change the smell in any atmosphere; it is profitable for doctrines that affect the way you live your life; it confronts and convicts you about areas that need to change in your life and gives you new ways of seeing things; it sets you straight and picks up those who have fallen flat in life and puts them back on their feet again; it provides instruction that is essential for you to live an upright life.**

The Scriptures Thoroughly Equip You

Paul went on to say that God has given us the Scriptures, "That the man of God may be perfect, thoroughly furnished unto all good works" (2 Timothy 3:17). The word "that" in this verse is the Greek word *hina*, and it means *in order that* and *points to a specific purpose*. The word "man" in Greek is the word *anthropos*, and it is a generic term for *a member of the human race, including both men and women*.

This brings us to the word "perfect" — the Greek word *artios*, which means *complete, mature, adequate, and completely sufficient in every way*. These words inform us that the Scriptures have *a specific purpose* for *each member of the human race* — every man and every woman. And that purpose includes making each of us *mature* and *completely sufficient in every way*.

Specifically, the Scriptures enable us to be "…thoroughly furnished unto all good works." The phrase "thoroughly furnished" is from the Greek word *exartidzo*, which means *to completely deck out* or *to fully supply* and *to fully equip*. It depicts *a ship that had previously been ill-equipped for traveling, but now has been loaded with new equipment and gear that enables it to sail anywhere.* Such boats were fully supplied, completely equipped, or thoroughly furnished. The word *exartidzo* depicts *a boat equipped to make it through all kinds of weather, including strong storms*; it is *a boat equipped for long-distance sailing.*

By using this word, the Holy Spirit is saying that as you open the Bible and begin to extract the life of God from its pages, it will begin to fully equip you to confront any situation that comes your way. Previously, you may have been ill-equipped for life, but as you open yourself to God's Word, it will supernaturally supply you with everything you need to make it through any storm and sail long distances. You will become "…thoroughly furnished unto all good works."

Putting the meanings of all these words together, here is the *Renner Interpretive Version* (*RIV*) of 2 Timothy 3:17:

> **…In order that any person belonging to God will be mature and sufficient in every way — completely outfitted with all the spiritual gear needed to equip anyone to sail long distances and through any type of spiritual storm or weather; it will enable anyone to bravely and nobly carry out all the good works that are needed to become a success in any sphere of life.**

Friend, that is what the Word of God will do in *your* life! Scripture is not just a book *about* God; God is actually in the Scripture. By reading and studying the Bible, you will release His life and power into yourself, transforming into His image. So don't delay — open the Bible today and start receiving the very life of God. Having a profound respect and reverence for Scripture is truly life-changing!

STUDY QUESTIONS

> **Study to shew thyself approved unto God, a workman that needeth not to be ashamed, rightly dividing the word of truth.**
> **— 2 Timothy 2:15**

1. There's no book on planet earth that compares with the Holy Bible. It was written in three different languages over the course of about 1,500 years by 40 different writers living on three different continents. Stop and ask yourself these questions: *How important is God's Word to me? If someone came and forcefully confiscated my Bible and all the Bibles in society, how would I react, and what kind of an impact would it have on my life?*

2. What puts God's Word in a class all its own? What will it provide you if you stick with it? Check out these passages for the answers:
   - Psalm 119:89; Matthew 5:18 and 24:35; 1 Peter 1:25
   - Psalm 119:103; Jeremiah 15:16; Job 23:12
   - Psalm 119:9; John 15:3 and 17:17; Ephesians 5:26
   - Romans 1:16; Hebrews 4:12; James 1:21

3. Take a few moments to carefully reflect on Second Peter 1:20 and 21. Why do you think this passage is vital for us to know — especially in the season of time in which we live?

PRACTICAL APPLICATION

**But be ye doers of the word, and not hearers only,
deceiving your own selves.
—James 1:22**

1. How about *you*? What is your *attitude* toward the Bible? Do you view it as the final *authority* in your life? Is reading and studying it *optional* or *indispensable*? If it is important to you, *when* and *how often* do you read it? What time of the day seems to be your best time to receive revelation from the Word? What happens inside of you as you read the Scriptures?

2. Second Timothy 3:16 says that the Scriptures are profitable for "reproof," which means the Word brings indisputable evidence and conviction of wrongdoing and gives you new ways of seeing things. In what specific areas of your life has the Word of God given you "reproof"?

3. God also gave us the Scriptures so we might be "…thoroughly furnished unto all good works" (2 Timothy 3:17). The phrase "thoroughly furnished" depicts a ship that had previously been ill-equipped for traveling, but now has been loaded with new equipment and gear

that enables it to sail anywhere. What are the top two areas of your life where you presently feel *ill-equipped*? Take some time to use a Bible concordance or an online search engine to find verses that will adequately equip you to deal with these areas.

TOPIC

Reverence for God in Tithes and Offerings

SCRIPTURES

1. **Matthew 6:21** — For where your treasure is, there will your heart be also.

2. **Malachi 1:6-14** — A son honoureth his father, and a servant his master: if then I be a father, where is mine honour? and if I be a master, where is my fear? saith the Lord of hosts unto you, O priests, that despise my name. And ye say, Wherein have we despised thy name? Ye offer polluted bread upon mine altar; and ye say, Wherein have we polluted thee? In that ye say, The table of the Lord is contemptible. And if ye offer the blind for sacrifice, is it not evil? and if ye offer the lame and sick, is it not evil? offer it now unto thy governor; will he be pleased with thee, or accept thy person? saith the Lord of hosts. And now, I pray you, beseech God that he will be gracious unto us: this hath been by your means: will he regard your persons? saith the Lord of hosts. Who is there even among you that would shut the doors for nought? neither do ye kindle fire on mine altar for nought. I have no pleasure in you, saith the Lord of hosts, neither will I accept an offering at your hand. For from the rising of the sun even unto the going down of the same my name shall be great among the Gentiles; and in every place incense shall be offered unto my name, and a pure offering: for my name shall be great among the heathen, saith the Lord of hosts. But ye have profaned it, in that ye say, The table of the Lord is polluted; and the fruit thereof, even his meat, is contemptible. Ye said also, Behold, what a weariness is it! and ye have snuffed at it, saith the Lord of hosts; and ye brought that which was torn, and the

lame, and the sick; thus ye brought an offering: should I accept this of your hand? saith the Lord. But cursed be the deceiver, which hath in his flock a male, and voweth, and sacrificeth unto the Lord a corrupt thing: for I am a great King, saith the Lord of hosts, and my name is dreadful among the heathen.

3. **Malachi 3:7-11** — Even from the days of your fathers ye are gone away from mine ordinances, and have not kept them. Return unto me, and I will return unto you, saith the Lord of hosts. But ye said, Wherein shall we return? Will a man rob God? Yet ye have robbed me. But ye say, Wherein have we robbed thee? In tithes and offerings. Ye are cursed with a curse: for ye have robbed me, even this whole nation. Bring ye all the tithes into the storehouse, that there may be meat in mine house, and prove me now herewith, saith the Lord of hosts, if I will not open you the windows of heaven, and pour you out a blessing, that there shall not be room enough to receive it. I will rebuke the devourer for your sakes, and he shall not destroy the fruits of your ground; neither shall your vine cast her fruit before the time in the field, saith the Lord of hosts.

4. **Genesis 7:11** — …the windows of heaven were opened….

5. **Genesis 7:19** — And the waters prevailed exceedingly upon the earth; and all the high hills, that were under the whole heaven, were covered.

6. **Exodus 16:4** — …Behold, I will rain bread from heaven for you…

7. **Psalm 78:23-25** — …opened the doors of heaven, and had rained down manna upon them to eat…and man did eat angels' food….

SYNOPSIS

For thousands of years, the Temple Mount in Jerusalem has been highly revered as a holy place. Just before the birth of Jesus, Herod the Great expanded the territory of the Temple Mount, erecting massive stones at the southern wall, which are very near to the Wailing Wall. Although many years have passed, devoted worshipers from across the globe still faithfully come to pray and honor the presence of God in this historical place.

What's interesting is that when the people of Israel came to enter into the presence of God, they never showed up empty-handed. They understood that when you enter into God's presence, you always brought a sacrifice or a gift. Thus, the local people would prepare their gifts and have them ready before they entered the temple. Travelers who were unable to carry a sacrifice on their long journey would stop at a local kiosk on the temple grounds and purchase a sacrifice to offer during their time of worship. They were serious about their giving, and there is much we can learn from their example.

Friend, God is the same yesterday, today, and forever (*see* Hebrews 13:8). Just as He desired and required His people to give then, He desires and requires us to give now. Indeed, giving touches His heart: "…For God loves (He takes pleasure in, prizes above other things, and is unwilling to abandon or do without) a cheerful (joyous, 'prompt to do it') giver [whose heart is in his giving]" (2 Corinthians 9:7 *AMPC*).

The emphasis of this lesson:

Your relationship with money reveals what you truly love. When you have a reverence for God in giving Him tithes and offerings, He opens the windows of Heaven and pours out uncontainable blessings in every area of your life.

Money Reveals the True Condition of Your Heart

Jesus taught more about money than many people realize — especially during His sermon on the mount. In fact, one of the most important verses on money is found in Matthew 6:21, which says, "For where your treasure is, there will your heart be also." In essence, He was saying, "What you do with your money reveals the condition of your heart. What you really love, you invest in." Therefore, if you want to know what a person really loves, follow their money.

It is easy to say, "Jesus, I love You," but then never demonstrate that love. Love gives. The Bible says, "For God so *loved* the world, that he *gave* his only begotten Son…" (John 3:16). Think of a man who constantly says to his wife, "I love you. I love you. I love you." But he spends virtually all his money on himself and never does anything special for his wife. His heart is fixated on himself, and that is where he puts his treasure.

Make no mistake: what you truly love, you invest in. If you love your spouse and your children, you give to them. If you love your church, you invest in it. Likewise, when you love the Lord, you give to Him the tithe and offering He has requested. When a person sacrificially gives as the Lord asks of him, that person demonstrates that his words of love for God are authentic. Where your treasure is, there your heart will be also.

The Israelites Were Bringing God Unacceptable Offerings

Next to Jesus' parables and teachings on giving, the book of Malachi has much to say on the topic. In chapter 1, we find God listening to His people as they spoke among themselves about bringing their gifts to Him. At that time, the people of Israel were not giving as they should and it showed. Through the prophet Malachi, God said, "Ye offer polluted bread upon mine altar; and ye say, Wherein have we polluted thee? In that ye say, The table of the Lord is contemptible" (Malachi 1:7).

Instead of giving to God with joyful hearts, the people were giving with resentment. Their loathsome attitude about giving their offerings had contaminated His altar. Basically, they were complaining and saying, "Oh, it's so hard to give. We just hate to do it." God, who is all-knowing, knew their thoughts and heard their conversations. Thus, He confronted them and said, "Your heart is wrong about your giving."

God continued His correction in verse 8 saying, "And if ye offer the blind for sacrifice, is it not evil? and if ye offer the lame and sick, is it not evil? offer it now unto thy governor; will he be pleased with thee, or accept thy person? saith the Lord of hosts." Essentially, God said, "You're bringing Me your blind, lame, and sick animals, are you? That's evil. Try bringing those kinds of animals to your governor. Do you think he'll accept it? Do you think he'll be pleased with you? I don't think so!"

Then in verse 10 God said, "Who is there even among you that would shut the doors for nought? neither do ye kindle fire on mine altar for nought. I have no pleasure in you, saith the Lord of hosts, neither will I accept an offering at your hand." In other words, God told them, "If this is the way you're going to treat Me, stop offering Me sacrifices altogether. Just shut the doors to the temple if you are going to dishonor Me so terribly."

Through Their Deception, They Came Under a Self-Imposed Curse

God's rebuke continued in verses 11 and 12. He declared, "For from the rising of the sun even unto the going down of the same my name shall be great among the Gentiles; and in every place incense shall be offered unto my name, and a pure offering: for my name shall be great among the heathen, saith the Lord of hosts. But ye have profaned it, in that ye say, The table of the Lord is polluted; and the fruit thereof, even his meat, is contemptible."

Here again, the people of Israel were murmuring and complaining about giving to God, saying it was too hard to give. God said, "You have profaned My Name by the polluted sacrifices you are offering Me. Your heart is not right. Nevertheless, My Name will be honored and made great among the heathens in the world."

To all this, God added in verse 13, "Ye said also, Behold, what a weariness is it! and ye have snuffed at it, saith the Lord of hosts; and ye brought that which was torn, and the lame, and the sick; thus ye brought an offering: should I accept this of your hand? saith the Lord." Once more, God called them out for bringing Him animals that were broken rejects. He said, "Sure, you're bringing me an offering, but is it really an offering? Is this what I'm supposed to accept from you?"

Then in verse 14, God vowed, "But cursed be the deceiver, which hath in his flock a male, and voweth, and sacrificeth unto the Lord a corrupt thing: for I am a great King, saith the Lord of hosts, and my name is dreadful among the heathen."

In essence, the people were saying they loved God and that they were bringing Him their best, but they weren't. God said, "You say you're bringing Me the best of your flocks, but you're not. Your best is still among your flock. You're actually bringing Me your worst and calling it your best. You are a bunch of liars, and because of your deception you are cursed." The people loved themselves more than they loved God. Thus their treasure — the healthy animals — were still in their own possession.

God Called Israel to Return to Him

Thankfully, God didn't abandon Israel for her corrupt ways. Instead, He called the people to *return* to Him and do the right thing. In Malachi 3:7, He said, "Even from the days of your fathers ye are gone away from mine ordinances, and have not kept them. Return unto me, and I will return unto you, saith the Lord of hosts. But ye said, Wherein shall we return?"

Here the people asked, "How are we to return to You, Lord?" He answered in Malachi 3:8 and 9:

"Will a man rob God? Yet ye have robbed me. But ye say, Wherein have we robbed thee? In tithes and offerings. Ye are cursed with a curse: for ye have robbed me, even this whole nation."

When the people of Israel clearly asked God what they had done wrong, He clearly answered them. He told them they had robbed Him by bringing Him the leftovers and the rejects of their flocks. They brought the sick, the lame, and the blind of their herds and kept the best for themselves. They had robbed God and withheld the choicest sacrifices, and God said, "You are cursed because of it."

To be clear: God did not curse them. Their decision to stop giving in obedience to Him removed them from the cycle of blessing and placed them under a curse. Again, the Scripture says, "Be not deceived; God is not mocked: for whatsoever a man soweth, that shall he also reap" (Galatians 6:7).

Did God need Israel's livestock or their money? No. He wanted their *heart*. What they were experiencing was more of a spiritual problem than a financial problem. Their choice to withhold their tithes and offerings was a manifestation of a spiritual sickness of the heart. The only way to make things right was to put God first in their lives and give Him what rightfully belonged to Him.

Does God need your money? No. He wants your heart. Jesus said, "Where your treasure is, there will your heart be also" (Matthew 6:21). When you obey God's command and put your money into His Kingdom, your heart will follow our money. It is your heart that God is after.

God Promised to 'Open the Windows of Heaven'

What was the remedy for Israel's calamity? God lovingly spelled out the solution in Malachi 3:10: "Bring ye all the tithes into the storehouse, that there may be meat in mine house, and prove me now herewith, saith the Lord of hosts, if I will not open you the windows of heaven, and pour you out a blessing, that there shall not be room enough to receive it."

God is so gracious and kind. He said, "If you will just do what you are supposed to do — if you will simply bring the tithe and the offering and give it into the Kingdom of God, investing it into the work of the ministry — your heart will be made right again. And when you do, I will open the windows of Heaven and pour out My blessings!"

The phrase "windows of Heaven" is very significant and is found in at least three other places in Scripture. It first appears in Genesis 7 during the days of Noah when God opened the *windows of Heaven* and poured out an unprecedented abundance of rain through them, covering the highest hills on earth with water (*see* vss. 11-24).

The second time we hear about the "windows of Heaven" is in the documented account of God's provision of manna (*see* Exodus 16). In Psalm 78:23-25, it says that God "...commanded the clouds from above, and *opened the doors of heaven*, and had rained down manna upon them [the people of Israel] to eat, and had given them of the corn of heaven. Man did eat angels' food...." For 40 years, bread poured through the open portals of Heaven for the people to eat. Rabbinical records estimate that 2,000 square cubits of manna, 50 to 60 cubits deep, rained from the sky every day. That is about 4,500 tons of manna a day, which is what scholars estimate would have been needed to feed the 3 million Israelites that were wandering through the desert. A 40-year supply of this much manna would have been approximately 65,700,000 tons!

This brings us to the third appearance of the words "windows of Heaven," which is Malachi 3:10. Again it says, "Bring ye all the tithes into the storehouse, that there may be meat in mine house, and prove me now herewith, saith the Lord of hosts, if I will not open you *the windows of heaven*, and pour you out a blessing, that there shall not be room enough to receive it."

To better grasp the magnitude of what God is promising here, we have to take into account the first two examples of Him opening the windows of Heaven. Every time that window (or door) of Heaven opens, miraculous things happen and abundance comes pouring through. In this case, God promises to open a window over generous givers and abundantly pour out immeasurable blessings on those who willingly give Him the tithe, or the tenth, of all their increase. The blessings will be so vast that the recipients will not have room enough to receive it.

Our obedience in giving is the key to the windows of Heaven. When we aren't giving, the windows are locked. However, when we are giving, the windows of Heaven are open, and God's abundance begins to pour into our lives.

Through Obedience, He Will Supply Our Every Need

What else has God promised to do if we would obediently give our tithe and offerings? In Malachi 3:11, He said, "And I will rebuke the devourer for your sakes, and he shall not destroy the fruits of your ground; neither shall your vine cast her fruit before the time in the field, saith the Lord of hosts."

When you open your hands to give, God opens His mouth to rebuke the devil. For those who give, God says to the devil, "Get off of them now! Move away from their finances, their health, and their relationships. They are obedient givers. I, the Lord, rebuke you for their sakes." When you open your hand to give, God opens His mouth and begins to rebuke the devourer for your sake. When you are generous with Him, He will be generous with you!

In Philippians 4, the apostle Paul wrote to the Church of Philippi, who had just sent him an extremely generous offering for his ministry work to continue. In response to their sacrificial giving, he encouraged them by saying, "But my God shall supply all your need according to his riches in glory by Christ Jesus" (vs. 19). This promise of God supplying all our needs is made to those who obediently give as the Philippian believers did.

Putting together the Greek meanings of the key words in this verse, here is the *Renner Interpretive Version* (*RIV*) of Philippians 4:19:

> **But my God will supply your needs so completely that He will eliminate all your deficiencies. He will meet all your physical and tangible needs until you are so full that you have no more capacity to hold anything else. He will supply all your needs until you are totally filled, packed full and overflowing to the point of bursting at the seams and spilling over.**

Again, when you are generous with God, God is generous with you. If you've been having financial difficulty or other problems in your life, the issue may be that you have unintentionally removed yourself from the sphere of God's blessing and, as a result, you are experiencing the devouring effects of the enemy in your life. If you have chosen not to give God the tithe, which biblically belongs to Him, you have removed yourself from the place of divine blessing.

Friend, God has an abundance of good things stored up for you that He wants to release in your life. If you've not been a giver, or had a reverence for God in tithes and offerings, why not start today? Begin by taking baby steps and give something to your church. The Bible says, "If you are willing and obedient, you shall eat the good of the land" (Isaiah 1:19 *NKJV*). God will honor your faith and will begin to bless your life in ways you never dreamed!

STUDY QUESTIONS

> **Study to shew thyself approved unto God, a workman that needeth not to be ashamed, rightly dividing the word of truth.**
> — 2 Timothy 2:15

1. Rick shared how he and his wife, Denise, went through severe financial hardship when he chose not to give their tithe and offering. He knew in his heart he was being disobedient, but he just didn't see how they could give and continue to feed their family and pay their bills. In what ways can you identify with Rick's story? What two things did he do that totally transformed their lives?

2. One thing Jesus talked about frequently was the subject of money. He knew that what is in a person's heart is often determined by what they do with their money. Take a few moments to read the story in Luke 21:1-4 about the poor widow who gave an offering at the temple. What is the Holy Spirit showing you in this story about *your* giving, the *size* of your gift, and how God observes what we give?

3. As a giver, God promises to "...supply all your need according to his riches in glory by Christ Jesus" (Philippians 4:19). What else does He promise you in Second Corinthians 9:6-11 as you obediently give? (Also consider Jesus' words in Luke 6:38.)

PRACTICAL APPLICATION

> **But be ye doers of the word, and not hearers only, deceiving your own selves.**
> — James 1:22

1. How would you describe your relationship with money? Are you a *giver* or a *hoarder*? Do you operate in *faith* or in *fear*? When you look

through the ledger of your checking account, what does it reveal about your heart and your treasure?

2. The Israelites said they loved God and that they were bringing Him their best offerings, but they weren't. They were actually bringing Him their defective, unwanted animals, and it grieved God greatly. Pause and pray, "Lord, am I giving You my best or my undesirable discards? Am I bringing You the first-fruits of what You bless me with or my leftovers? Have I withheld something that rightfully belongs to You? Do I really demonstrate my love for You in my giving, or have I deceived myself?" *Listen.* What is the Holy Spirit speaking to you? Repent of any disobedience He shows you, and begin taking steps to make things right in the area of your giving.

LESSON 5

TOPIC

Reverence for God in His People

SCRIPTURES

1. **1 Corinthians 3:16, 17** — Know ye not that ye are the temple of God, and that the Spirit of God dwelleth in you? If any man defile the temple of God, him shall God destroy; for the temple of God is holy, which temple ye are.

2. **Ephesians 2:19, 20, 22** — Now therefore ye are no more strangers and foreigners, but fellowcitizens with the saints, and of the household of God; and are built upon the foundation of the apostles and prophets, Jesus Christ himself being the chief corner stone; in whom ye also are builded together for an habitation of God through the Spirit.

3. **1 Corinthians 12:12, 13** — For as the body is one, and hath many members, and all the members of that one body, being many, are one body; so also is Christ. For by one Spirit are we all baptized into one body, whether we be Jews or Gentiles, whether we be bond or free; and have been all made to drink into one Spirit.

4. **Galatians 3:28** — There is neither Jew nor Greek, there is neither bond nor free, there is neither male nor female; for ye are all one in Christ Jesus.

5. **Colossians 3:11** — Where there is neither Greek nor Jew, circumcision nor uncircumcision, Barbarian, Scythian, bond nor free; but Christ is all, and in all.

6. **1 Corinthians 12:27** — Now ye are the body of Christ, and members in particular"

GREEK WORDS

1. "know" — **οἶδα** (*oida*): to perceive, understand, or comprehend

2. "temple" — **ναός** (*naos*): a temple or a highly decorated shrine; it presents the image of vaulted ceilings, marble, granite, gold, silver, and highly decorated ornamentation; pictures the most sacred, innermost part of a temple; the Holy of Holies

3. "dwelleth" — **οἰκέω** (*oikeo*): to dwell in; to take up residency; pictures a habitation; a home; a permanent place of residence; to settle down; to make one's home

4. "defile" — **φθείρω** (*phtheiro*): to corrupt, destroy, or spoil; to perish or waste away; to bring into a place of degeneration, deterioration or decomposition; to move downward from a higher level to a lower level

5. "destroy" — **φθείρω** (*phtheiro*): to corrupt, destroy, or spoil; to perish or waste away; to bring into a place of degeneration, deterioration or decomposition; to move downward from a higher level to a lower level

6. "strangers" — **ξένος** (*xenos*): one from the outside; a foreigner, alien, or stranger

7. "foreigners" — **πάροικος** (*paroikos*): from **παρά** (*para*) and **οἶκος** (*oikos*); the word **παρά** (*para*) means "alongside" or "on the exterior"; the word **οἶκος** (*oikos*) means "a house"; compounded, the new word depicts one who is on the exterior; one who is outside of the house; one who does not belong to the family; a non-citizen with few legal rights

8. "fellowcitizens" — **συμπολίτης** (*sumpolites*): from **σύν** (*sun*) and **πολίτης** (*polites*); the word **σύν** (*sun*) means "together with"; the word **πολίτης** (*polites*) means "a citizen or resident of a city"; compounded, the new word depicts one who possesses citizenship along with other

citizens; pictures people with citizenship who possess the legal rights that accompany citizenship

9. "saints" — ἅγιος (*hagios*): holy; consecrated; different; separate; to be treated as holy

10. "household" — οἰκεῖος (*oikeios*): belonging to a house or family; domestic; intimate family membership; related by blood; kindred; real members of a family and related by blood

11. "builded together" — συνοικοδομέω (*sunoikodomeo*): being built together; to jointly build together; to make one of many parts

12. "habitation" — κατοικητήριον (*katoiketerion*): from κατοικέω, a compound of κατά (*kata*), meaning "down," and οἰκέω (*oikeo*) meaning "to dwell or to reside in a house"; one who settles down into a residence and makes himself to feel comfortable and at home; permanent residency

13. "Jews or Gentiles" — Jews generally loathed Gentiles and deemed them vile and unclean; Gentiles generally viewed Jews as narrow-minded bigots; these two groups were divided in society and felt deep prejudice toward each other

14. "bond or free" — the "bond" and "free" lived in different spheres of society and rarely interfaced with one another; these were socially opposed to each other

15. "male nor female" — in both the Jewish and Gentile worlds, women did not have the same rights as men; women were not allowed in public meetings, could generally not own property, and had fewer legal rights; while honored in the home, in society, women were generally deemed inferior to men

16. "Barbarian, Scythian" — the word "barbarian" means one whose speech is rude, rough, harsh; one who speaks a foreign or strange language that is not understood by another; any foreigner ignorant of the Greek language and the Greek culture, hence one lacking culture and deemed to be uncivilized and rude; the word "Scythian" refers to a specific people group deemed to be the lowest level of all barbarians; even "barbarians" had prejudices against other barbarians, and most barbarians thought they were better than Scythians, who were viewed to be uncontrollable, incorrigible deplorables

17. "all, and in all" — πάντα καὶ ἐν πᾶσιν (*panta kai en pansin*): an all-embracing phrase that leaves none out and levels the playing field

in Christ between all ethnicity, genders, languages, races, colors, and nationalities

18. "drink" — πίνω (*pino*): to drink; to consume; pictures one who consumes some type of drink

19. "members" — μέλος (*melos*): a member of the human body; members that belong to the whole

20. "in particular" — μέρος (*meros*): in particular; with an assigned position; having a lot or destiny

SYNOPSIS

In Old Testament times, the Spirit of God dwelt in the innermost part of the temple — a place that was called the Holy of Holies. Today, *we are the temple for God's Spirit*, and He has chosen to take up permanent residence inside of us. Our body is His dwelling place. Thus, every believer is a walking, talking sanctuary of the Living God. Although we come from many different cultures, live on different continents, and speak different languages, we are all a vital part of the Body of Christ. We are filled with the same Holy Spirit and God has blended us all together in the same household of faith. Therefore, we need to learn how to develop a sincere reverence for God in His people.

The emphasis of this lesson:

Every believer — regardless of skin color, ethnic background, language, or culture — is an integral part of the temple of God. Individually and corporately, we house the presence of God, and we need to have a reverential fear of God in how we treat one another.

Individually and Corporately, We Are God's Temple

First Corinthians 3:16 says, "Know ye not that ye are the temple of God, and that the Spirit of God dwelleth in you?" The word "know" here is the Greek word *oida*, which means to perceive, understand, or comprehend; it is knowledge gained by personal experience or personal observation. The word "temple" is the Greek word *naos*, and it describes *a temple* or *a highly decorated shrine*; *it presents the image of vaulted ceilings, marble, granite, gold, silver, and highly decorated ornamentation.* It pictures *the most sacred, innermost part of a temple* and was the word used to depict the Holy of Holies.

Interestingly, the apostle Paul chose this word to describe us — Christ's Church. We are God's habitation in which He "dwelleth." The word "dwelleth" is the Greek word *oikeo*, which means *to dwell in* or *to take up residency*. It pictures *a habitation, a home*, or *a permanent place of residence*. It carries the idea of settling down and making oneself feel at home. Hence, God is not a temporary visitor; He has moved into each member of the Body of Christ, and we need to be careful how we treat the people that make up His temple.

Paul went on to say, "If any man defile the temple of God, him shall God destroy; for the temple of God is holy, which temple ye are" (1 Corinthians 3:17). What is interesting is that the words "defile" and "destroy" are the same word in Greek — the word *phtheiro*, which means *to corrupt, to destroy*, or *to spoil; to perish or waste away*. It can also mean *to bring into a place of degeneration, deterioration, or decomposition; to move downward from a higher level to a lower level*. By using the word *phtheiro*, Paul was saying that if anyone mishandles the temple of God, treating His people in such a way that brings them into corruption, decomposition, or deterioration, God will destroy him. In other words, the way we treat the Church — and its members — is the way God is going to treat us.

We Are 'Fellow Citizens' in God's 'Household'

The idea of oneness in the Body of Christ and us being the temple of the Holy Spirit is a theme woven all throughout the New Testament. Take Ephesians 2:19, for example. It says, "Now therefore ye are no more strangers and foreigners, but fellowcitizens with the saints, and of the household of God."

This verse makes us aware that we are not alone in our journey of faith. We are joined by everyone else who has called on the name of the Lord and is saved. In fact, it says we are no more "strangers and foreigners." The word "strangers" is the Greek word *xenos*, and it describes *one from the outside; a foreigner, alien*, or *stranger*. The word "foreigners" is the Greek word *paroikos*, which is a compound of the word *para*, meaning *alongside* or *on the exterior*, and the word *oikos*, meaning *a house*. When these words are compounded, the new word — *paroikos* — depicts *one who is on the exterior; one who is outside of the house; one who does not belong to the family; a non-citizen with few legal rights*.

So as a believer, you are no longer on the exterior of God's temple or on the outside of His family. On the contrary, you are *inside* His family. More specifically, the Bible says you are "fellowcitizens with the saints." The word "fellowcitizens" is the Greek word *sumpolites*. It is a compound of the word *sun*, which means *together with*, and the word *polites*, which describes *a citizen or resident of a city*. When these words are compounded to form the word *sumpolites*, it depicts *one who possesses citizenship along with other citizens*; it pictures *people with citizenship who possess the legal rights that accompany citizenship*.

Essentially, Paul said, "There was a time when you were a stranger or foreigner living outside the family of God. But through your faith in Christ, you have been joined to others — you are a fellow citizen with the 'saints.'" The word "saints" is a translation of the Greek word *hagios*, which means *holy, consecrated, different*, or *separate*. "Saints" are people whose lives have been touched and filled with God's presence, and as a result their status is forever changed. They are separated, sanctified, and to be treated as holy.

As "fellow citizens" and "saints," the Bible says you are part of "the household of God" (Ephesians 2:19). The word "household" is the Greek word *oikeios*, which means *belonging to a house or family; domestic by nature; intimate family membership*. This word describes *those who are kindred* or *real members of a family that are related by blood*. Friend, the blood of Jesus has brought us together from different languages and different backgrounds into one family. We are the household of God "and are built upon the foundation of the apostles and prophets, Jesus Christ himself being the chief corner stone" (Ephesians 2:20).

Verse 22 goes on to say, "In whom ye also are builded together for an habitation of God through the Spirit." The phrase "builded together" is the Greek word *sunoikodomeo*, which literally means *being built together; to jointly build together* or *to make one of many parts*. Again, this speaks of why we need to have reverence for God in others. He has brought us together and supernaturally connected us, and we have become His "habitation."

The word "habitation" is the Greek word *katoiketerion*, which is a compound of the word *kata*, meaning *down*, and *oikeo*, meaning *to dwell* or *to reside in a house*. When compounded to form the word *katoiketerion*, it describes *one who settles down into a residence and makes himself to feel comfortable and at home*; it is *a permanent residency*.

We Are Many Parts But One Body

One of the best illustrations of the great diversity in the Body of Christ is found in First Corinthians 12. In verses 12 and 13, Paul wrote, "For as the body is one, and hath many members, and all the members of that one body, being many, are one body; so also is Christ. For by one Spirit are we all baptized into one body, whether we be Jews or Gentiles, whether we be bond or free; and have been all made to drink into one Spirit."

Notice he says **"whether we be Jews or Gentiles."** Jews generally loathed Gentiles and deemed them vile and unclean. Likewise, Gentiles generally viewed Jews as narrow-minded bigots. These two groups were divided in society and felt deep prejudice toward each other. You would have never found them in the same church or seated at the same table having a meal together. Nevertheless, in Christ, it no longer matters if you're a Jew or Gentile. You're all washed by the same precious Blood of Jesus and members of the same household of faith.

Paul also said it doesn't matter **"whether we be bond or free."** The "bond" and "free" were another distinct classification in society, and they were very different from each other. As a rule, the "bond" and the "free" did not mingle. In fact, they were socially opposed to each other. Yet in this passage, Paul removed the wall of separation between these two groups and said we "…have been all made to drink into one Spirit."

God reiterates the dissolution of these class distinctions in Galatians 3:28, saying, "There is neither Jew nor Greek, there is neither bond nor free, there is neither male nor female: for ye are all one in Christ Jesus." In addition to the "Jew or Greek" (Gentile) and "bond or free" classifications, Paul added **"neither male nor female."**

In both the Jewish and Gentile worlds, women did not have the same rights as men. Specifically, women were not allowed in public meetings, they could generally not own property, and they had fewer legal rights. Even though women were honored in the home, men generally viewed themselves as superior to women in society. Yet in Christ, the "male/female" distinction disappears. For Paul to make the statement that there is "neither male nor female" in Christ was absolutely audacious!

Moreover, in Colossians 3:11, Paul expanded the termination of societal classifications even further by including **barbarians and Scythians**. He said, "…there is neither Greek nor Jew, circumcision nor uncircumcision, *Barbarian, Scythian*, bond nor free; but Christ is all, and in all."

The word "barbarian" means *one whose speech is rude, rough, harsh; one who speaks a foreign or strange language which is not understood by another.* This included *any foreigner ignorant of the Greek language and the Greek culture, hence one lacking culture and deemed to be uncivilized and rude.* This brings us to the word "Scythian," which refers to *a specific people group deemed to be the lowest level of all barbarians.* As strange as it may seem, even "barbarians" had prejudices against other barbarians; most barbarians thought they were better than Scythians, who were viewed to be uncontrollable, incorrigible, deplorables. Speaking through Paul, the Holy Spirit said that in Christ, even the class distinction between barbarian and Scythian is dissolved.

How Does All This Apply to Us Today?

Think about it. As a part of the household of God, there is no such thing as a Spanish church and an English church, a white church and a black church, or an Eastern church and a Western church. There is only *one* Church — the Church of the Lord Jesus Christ that is washed in His Blood, filled with His Spirit, healed by His stripes, and empowered by His Name!

Instead of getting angry and offended over the differences in the people in the Body of Christ, learn to appreciate and celebrate them. God wants you to reverence His presence in *all* His people. He said, "Now ye are the body of Christ, and members in particular" (1 Corinthians 12:27). The word "members" is the Greek word *melos*, which describes *a member of the human body; members that belong to the whole.* Again, this signifies that we do not belong to ourselves; we are interconnected with other believers. *The phrase* "in particular" is a translation of the Greek word *meros*, which means *in particular; with an assigned position; those having a lot or destiny.*

This passage tells us it doesn't matter what language we speak, what color skin tone we have, or the culture in which we were raised. God has marvelously washed us in the blood of Jesus, forgiven our sins, and translated us into the family of God. All of us have been made to drink of the self-same Holy Spirit and we all have a specific destiny in the household of God.

STUDY QUESTIONS

**Study to shew thyself approved unto God, a workman that
needeth not to be ashamed, rightly dividing the word of truth.
— 2 Timothy 2:15**

1. When it comes to God's dealings with mankind, there is a repeated principle found in Acts 10:34 and 35; Romans 2:11 and 10:12; Galatians 2:6 and Ephesians 6:9. What is this truth? Why do you think it is important for us to remember this?

2. In First Corinthians 3:17, Paul informed us that the way we treat the Church — and its members — is the way God is going to treat us. What is the most important thing God requires you to do for all fellow Christians? (*See* Ephesians 4:32; Colossians 3:13; Matthew 6:14, 15; Mark 11:25.) What will happen if you willfully chose not to obey this instruction?

3. Are you having a hard time doing this for anyone in particular? If so, who is it and what did they do? Take time now to pray, asking God to forgive you for holding onto their offense and for His power to forgive them and bless them as He tells us to do (*see* 1 Peter 3:8, 9).

PRACTICAL APPLICATION

**But be ye doers of the word, and not hearers only,
deceiving your own selves.
— James 1:22**

1. Is there a Christian you know or a certain person at your church that you are struggling to accept? What is it about them that is offensive and that seems to rub you the wrong way? How is this lesson helping you see this person (and others in the Body of Christ) differently?

2. Pray and ask God to give you a sincere reverence for His presence in others. Say, "Lord, please forgive me for being narrow-minded and erroneously thinking that everyone should think and act and worship you exactly like me. Open my eyes to see and appreciate the wonderful differences in the Body of Christ and reverence Your Spirit living in them. In Jesus' name, Amen."